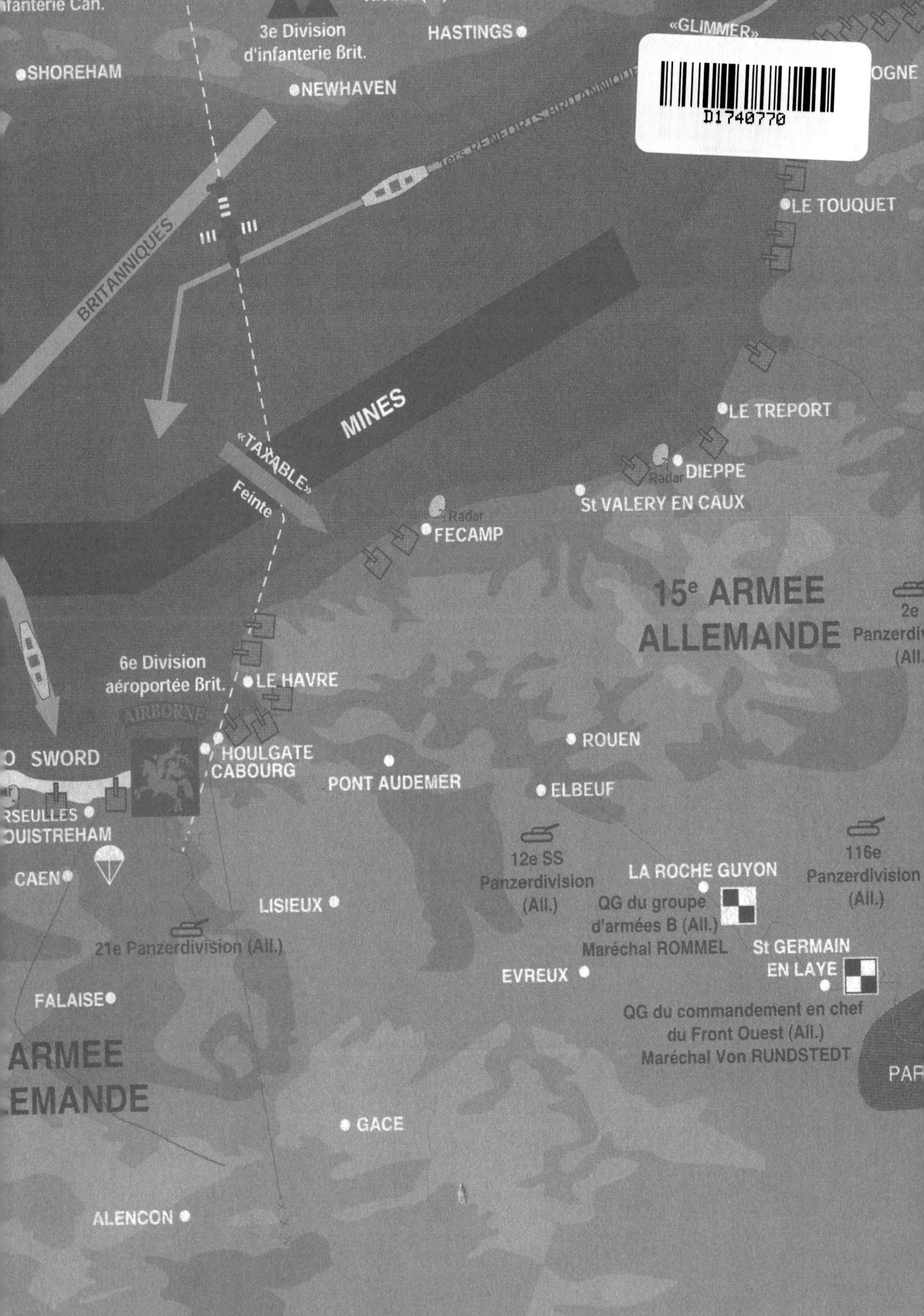

3e Division
d'infanterie Brit.

HASTINGS

«GLIMMER»

OGNE

SHOREHAM

NEWHAVEN

LE TOUQUET

BRITANNIQUES

MINES

«TAXABLE»

Feinte

LE TREPORT

Radar

DIEPPE

St VALERY EN CAUX

Radar

FECAMP

15e ARMEE
ALLEMANDE

2e
Panzerdi
(All.)

6e Division
aéroportée Brit.

LE HAVRE

AIRBORNE

ROUEN

SWORD

HOULGATE
CABOURG

ELBEUF

SEULLES

PONT AUDEMER

OUISTREHAM

12e SS
Panzerdivision
(All.)

LA ROCHE GUYON

116e
Panzerdivision
(All.)

CAEN

LISIEUX

QG du groupe
d'armées B (All.)
Maréchal ROMMEL

St GERMAIN
EN LAYE

21e Panzerdivision (All.)

EVREUX

FALAISE

QG du commandement en chef
du Front Ouest (All.)
Maréchal Von RUNDSTEDT

ARMEE

PAR

EMANDE

GACE

ALENCON

NORMANDY JUNE 44

SWORD BEACH
CAEN

SCRIPT: **JEAN-BLAISE DJIAN**
AND **ISABELLE BOURNIER**
DRAWING: **BRUNO MARIVAIN**
COLOURS: **CATHERINE MOREAU**
DOSSIER: **ISABELLE BOURNIER**

OREP EDITIONS

We would like to thank Daniel DANOY from Ouistreham for his advice and friendship.
Jean-Blaise

© OREP Éditions

First published in France in May 2012 - Legal deposit: 3rd quarter 2016
Translation: Adeline Adams
ISBN 978-2-8151-0332-9

June 5th 2009, La Cambe Cemetery. Following the German government's initiative, a reconciliation ceremony is being held in three languages in front of veterans of different nationalities. His excellence, Ambassador Schaefers, is addressing everyone...

To have a future, one must know the past. This universal quote from Wilhelm von Humboldt doesn't know any more boundaries...

... Than the feelings linking us between German, French, American, Australian, British, Canadian, Finnish...

... Polish and Norwegian, come together today at La Cambe. These feelings and thoughts never stop assailing us...

... In every military cemetery of the great continental conflicts of the past century.

And yet, this is a special place: it's a German cemetery from World War II.

German was the language of the occupying forces. They came from Germany and they executed the orders of a government...

... To which they owed fidelity and obedience in the name of Germany. The Germans were the enemy.

1

3

YOU WILL THEREFORE UNDERSTAND THAT WE, GERMANS, STILL HAVE MIXED FEELINGS TODAY WHEN WE COME INTO THIS PLACE...

...EVEN IF THE TIME HAS COME FOR US NOW TO BE FRIENDS AND TO STAND TOGETHER WITH OUR FORMER ENEMIES.

THAT'S WHY TODAY'S CEREMONY ISN'T ADDRESSING THE NATIONS, EVEN IF WE'LL HEAR THE NATIONAL HYMNS AT THE END OF IT.

WE ARE ADDRESSING THE GENERATIONS WHO HAVE GATHERED HERE TODAY.

LET'S ACT TOGETHER, JUST LIKE WILHELM VON HUMBOLDT WOULD HAVE.

THANK YOU.

SHALL WE GO AND REST AT THE HOTEL BEFORE THIS EVENING'S DINNER, GRANDPA...

NO

WHAT DO YOU MEAN, NO ?

I NEED TO GO TO OUISTREHAM.

2

WHAT DO YOU WANT TO DO AT OUISTREHAM ?

I NEED TO SEE SOMEONE...

WHO ?

A FRIEND... YOU DON'T KNOW HIM KAREN, IT'S THE FIRST TIME YOU HAVE COME HERE...

DING DONG

Helene et Paul RAPIER

WOLFY ? IS THAT YOU WOLFY ?

I... I DIDN'T HAVE TIME TO INFORM YOU... PAUL WASN'T FEELING THAT WELL LATELY... HE LEFT US TWO WEEKS AGO...

3

DON'T MOVE, I'LL CARRY THIS IN THE KITCHEN AND BRING YOU SOME CALVA*...

EXCUSE ME HELEN... I WAS WONDERING... HAVE PAUL AND GRANDPA KNOWN EACH OTHER FOR A LONG TIME?

SIXTY-FIVE YEARS. THEY MET DURING THE LANDING IN JUNE 1944, HERE, IN OUISTREHAM...

COULD YOU TELL ME HOW AND WHY THEY WERE SO CLOSE? BECAUSE, FOR ME, HIS GRANDDAUGHTER, IT'S A BIG MYSTERY... HE NEVER MENTIONS ANYTHING ABOUT IT...

ALL RIGHT, BUT I CAN ONLY TELL YOU WHAT I KNOW DEAR...

IN 1942, PAUL, WHOM I DIDN'T KNOW YET, WAS PART OF THE RESISTANCE. IN THE AUTUMN OF THAT SAME YEAR, AFTER AN OPERATION THAT DIDN'T TURN OUT WELL...

* APPLE BRANDY

4

... HE MANAGED TO JOIN THE FREE FRENCH FORCES OF GENERAL DE GAULLE IN LONDON.

IN DECEMBER, HE JOINS MAJOR KIEFFER IN THE 10TH INTER-ALLIED COMMANDO... IN CRICCIETH, IN WALES, IF I REMEMBER WELL...

AFTER TWO MONTHS AT THE ACHNACARRY COMMANDO SCHOOL, IN SCOTLAND, WHERE HE MEETS BILL MILLIN*...

... HE TRAVELS BACK TO THE SOUTH OF ENGLAND.

AGAIN, THE TRAINING IS PARTICULARLY INTENSIVE.

HE EVEN TAKES PART IN SEVERAL NIGHT RAIDS ON THE FRENCH COAST.

* SOLDIER OF THE FIRST SPECIAL SERVICE BRIGADE COMMANDED BY LORD LOVAT. HE LANDED IN THE MIDDLE OF THE FIGHTERS WITH HIS BAGPIPES AS HIS ONLY WEAPON... 5

HE THEN PARTICIPATES IN A LAST BIG OPERATION IN NAIRN, SCOTLAND, IN WHICH HE INTEGRATES INTO THE 4TH COMMANDO... I REMEMBER, HE WAS SO PROUD ABOUT IT...

IN APRIL 1944, HE GOES BACK TO THE SOUTH OF ENGLAND, IN BEXHILL, I THINK...

AFTERWARDS, THE COMMANDOS GO BACK TO SOUTHAMPTON. THE INHABITANTS GIVE THEM A WARM WELCOME, WHICH MOTIVATES THEM.

THEY THEN ARRIVE IN A VERY SEVERE AMERICAN MILITARY CAMP: NOTHING ALLOWED, NO LETTERS, NO CONTACT WITH THE OUTSIDE WORLD... THEY ARE TOLD ABOUT THEIR MISSION BUT NOT THEIR DESTINATION...

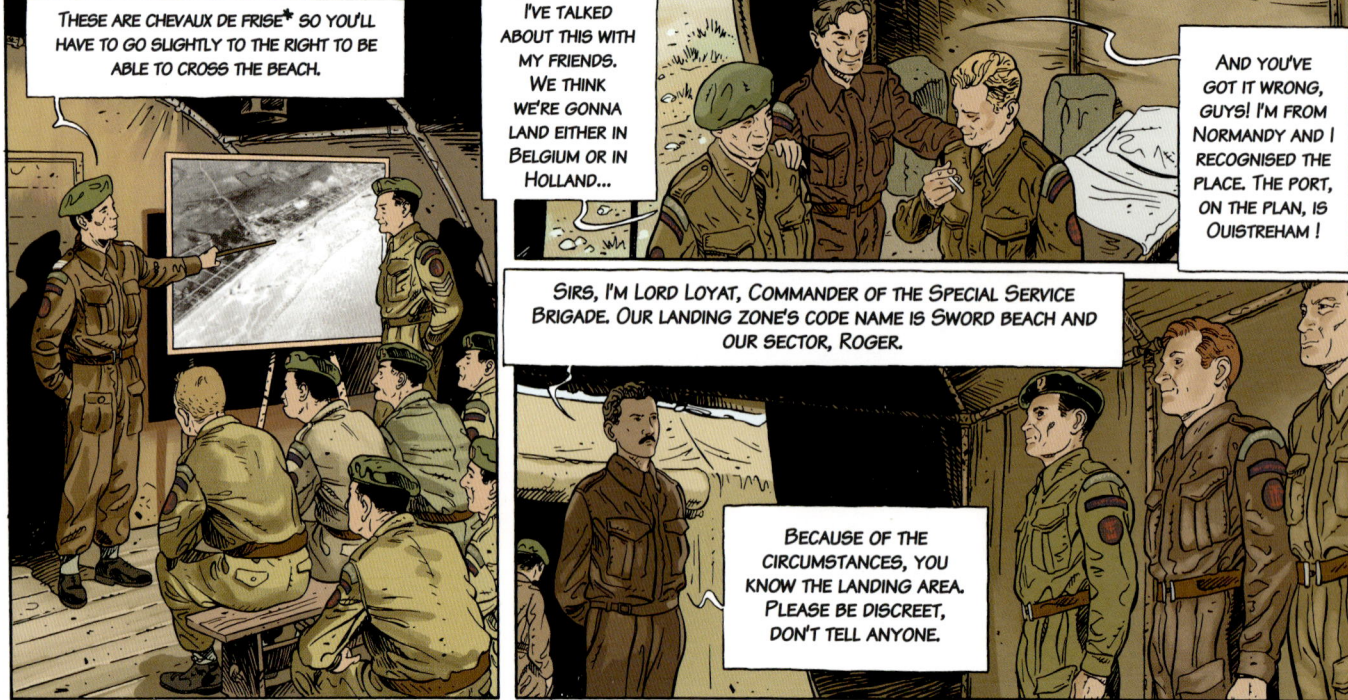

THESE ARE CHEVAUX DE FRISE* SO YOU'LL HAVE TO GO SLIGHTLY TO THE RIGHT TO BE ABLE TO CROSS THE BEACH.

I'VE TALKED ABOUT THIS WITH MY FRIENDS. WE THINK WE'RE GONNA LAND EITHER IN BELGIUM OR IN HOLLAND...

AND YOU'VE GOT IT WRONG, GUYS! I'M FROM NORMANDY AND I RECOGNISED THE PLACE. THE PORT, ON THE PLAN, IS OUISTREHAM !

SIRS, I'M LORD LOYAT, COMMANDER OF THE SPECIAL SERVICE BRIGADE. OUR LANDING ZONE'S CODE NAME IS SWORD BEACH AND OUR SECTOR, ROGER.

BECAUSE OF THE CIRCUMSTANCES, YOU KNOW THE LANDING AREA. PLEASE BE DISCREET, DON'T TELL ANYONE.

* MEDIEVAL DEFENSIVE OBSTACLE CONSISTING OF A PORTABLE FRAME COVERED WITH MANY PROJECTING LONG IRON OR WOODEN SPIKES

6

THEY'RE REALLY DRIVING US UP THE WALL SINCE LAST SUMMER: ONE DAY YES, THE OTHER DAY NO... IT WAS SUPPOSED TO BE IN THE SPRING...

YOU KNOW WHAT THE BRITISH ARE! THEY CAN KEEP SECRETS BETTER THAN ANYONE...

YES, WELL, NOW, THEY COULD TELL US!

I MEAN IT! ALL THESE AREAS ARE FORBIDDEN TO FOREIGNERS... IN THE TRAIN STATIONS, THE MILITARY POLICE ARE ASKING FOR EVERY CITIZEN'S IDENTITY CARD, AND EVERY SOLDIER'S PASS...

THEY SHUT US UP IN THIS CAMP* FOR SECURITY REASONS, BUT ALSO SO THAT WE COULD GET SOME REST. WE HAVE NO CHORES TO DO, NOTHING...

YES, I FEEL LIKE I'M ON HOLIDAY... DRINKING, EATING, GOING TO THE MOVIES... BUT WE'RE CUT OFF FROM THE WORLD!

CAREFUL GUYS, THIS CASINO** HAS BEEN CHANGED INTO A BLOCKHOUSE...

THEY FORBID US TO TALK ABOUT IT, BUT I RECOGNISED IT; IT'S OUISTREHAM'S CASINO...

DID YOU SEE THAT, THEY GAVE OUT LEAFLETS IN ENGLISH TO ALL THE TASK FORCE. I SPEAK ENGLISH SO I COULD READ THEM...

AND SO, WHAT DOES IT SAY?

THAT WE'RE NOT CONQUERORS BUT SOLDIERS COMING TO FREE THEIR ALLIED PRISONERS.

IT ALSO MENTIONS THE ATTITUDE WE NEED TO HAVE TOWARDS FRENCH WOMEN...

* TICHFIELD CAMP, NEAR FAREHAM, FACING THE ISLE OF WIGHT.
** THE NAMES WRITTEN ON THE MAP ARE IN POLISH OR RUSSIAN TO KEEP THE SECRET...

7

SIRS, WE'RE GONNA GIVE OUT GENERAL EISENHOWER'S* AGENDA FOR THE DAY. READ IT CAREFULLY.

YOU'RE ABOUT TO EMBARK ON A GREAT CRUSADE THAT WE HAVE BEEN WORKING ON FOR MANY MONTHS. THE WORLD IS WATCHING YOU...

ALL THE TIME, HOPE AND PRAYERS FROM ALL THE PEOPLE WITH A GREAT LOVE OF LIBERTY ACCOMPANY YOU. TOGETHER WITH OUR BRAVE ALLIES AND OUR BROTHERS IN ARMS FROM THE OTHER FRONTS...

YOU'LL MANAGE TO DESTROY THE GERMAN MACHINE OF WAR AND TO ELIMINATE THE NAZI TYRANNY THAT WEIGHS HEAVY ON THE PEOPLE OF OPPRESSED EUROPE...

... AND YOU'LL ASSURE YOUR OWN SECURITY IN A FREE WORLD.

THE MISSION YOU'RE ASKED TO DO ISN'T AN EASY ONE. YOU'RE GONNA DEAL WITH A WELL TRAINED AND WELL EQUIPPED ENEMY THAT HAS ALSO BEEN REINFORCED BY THE FIGHTING. THEY WILL FIGHT RUTHLESSLY.

BUT WE'RE IN 1944. SO MANY THINGS HAVE HAPPENED SINCE THE NAZI TRIUMPHS OF 1940-41.

THE UNITED NATIONS HAVE INFLICTED HEAVY DEFEATS TO THE GERMANS DURING PITCHED BATTLES, MAN TO MAN.

* SUPREME COMMANDER OF THE ALLIED EXPEDITIONARY FORCES.

8

OUR AERIAL DEFENSE HAS CONSIDERABLY REDUCED THE ENEMY'S STRENGTH IN THE AIR AND THEIR POSSIBLE ATTACKS ON THE GROUND.

WE ARE WELL IN ADVANCE WITH WEAPONS AND AMMUNITION THANKS TO OUR INTERIOR FRONT, AND THEY HAVE PUT WELL-TRAINED COMBATANTS AT OUR DISPOSAL.

THE WIND HAS CHANGED. FREE MEN FROM ALL OVER THE WORLD ARE WALKING TOWARDS VICTORY.

I ENTIRELY TRUST YOUR COURAGE, YOUR SENSE OF DUTY, YOUR QUALITIES AS SOLDIERS.

OUR ONLY GOAL CAN'T BE ANYTHING OTHER THAN A FULL VICTORY. GOOD LUCK.

LET'S ASK OUR ALMIGHTY GOD TO BLESS THIS NOBLE AND GREAT ENTERPRISE. GENERAL EISENHOWER.

ON JUNE 3RD, AROUND 2AM, WHEREAS EVERYONE IS EITHER SLEEPING TO BE FRESH, OR IS CLEANING HIS WEAPON SO IT DOESN'T FAIL AT THE FATEFUL MOMENT...

THE SEA IS TOO BAD, GUYS! WE'RE NOT LEAVING TONIGHT ANYMORE. DEPARTURE HAS BEEN POSTPONED...

AROUND 5PM, THE BATTALION'S CHAPLAIN IS CELEBRATING MASS. A LOT OF ENGLISH CATHOLICS ARE ATTENDING TOO...

9

THE NIGHT IS THROUGH BUT THE WEATHER ISN'T MUCH BETTER... ON THE CONTRARY. ARE THEY GONNA POSTPONE AGAIN?

I HAVE A BAD FEELING... EVERYTHING IS AGAINST US...

MY FRIENDS, THE WEATHER ISN'T FAVORABLE FOR US. BUT TODAY WILL STILL BE THE BIG DAY...

A FEW HOURS BEFORE LEAVING THE CAMP, LORD LOVAT GATHERS ALL THE OFFICERS OF THE FIRST SPECIAL SERVICE BRIGADE...

SIRS, THE SUCCESS OF THIS LANDING DEPENDS ON THE ESTABLISHMENT OF THE BRIDGEHEADS...

WE GAVE THIS IMPORTANT MISSION TO OUR COMMANDOS AND PARATROOPERS. WE CANNOT FAIL.

PACKED TOGETHER, THE FRENCH ARE LAUGHING, SINGING AND CALLING OUT ON PASSERSBY...

THE TRUCKS FINALLY STAY STILL IN WARSASH'S PORT, NEAR SOUTHAMPTON.

10

BEFORE THEY EMBARK, THE MEN SPEND AN HOUR CHECKING THEIR GRENADES AND EXPLOSIVES...

HERE, TAKE THIS BOARDING CARD! IT HAS TWO TICKETS WITH YOUR NAME, YOUR REGIMENTAL NUMBER AND THE NUMBER OF YOUR UNIT.

ONE IS FOR GOING THERE, THE OTHER TO COME BACK IN CASE YOU'RE INJURED AND UNCONSCIOUS...

THE WEATHER'S AWFUL! THIS COLD WILL KILL US IF WE HAVE TO JUMP IN THE WATER FAR FROM THE BEACH...

22H56, ENGLISH TIME. TWO HALIFAX* BOMBERS TAKE OFF FROM TARRANT RUSHTON'S BASE, NEAR EXETER. EACH OF THEM SHOOTS TWO HORSA GLIDERS AT THE END OF 350 FEET OF CABLE...

THE WIND IS BLOWING IN GUSTS OF 80 TO 90 KM AN HOUR.

* ONE FLOWN BY STODLEY, THE OTHER BY WALLROCK. STODLEY'S MISSION IS TO BOMB CAEN'S CEMENT WORKS AFTER HE'S LAUNCHED THE GLIDERS IN ORDER TO CREATE A DIVERSION.

THE GLIDERS ARE OVERLOADED! WITH THIS WEATHER, THEY'LL HAVE TROUBLE LANDING AT MORE THAN 130 KM PER HOUR... THERE IS A GREAT CHANCE THAT THE MEN* WILL DIE...

SHUT UP, JOHN! THEIR MISSION IS TO CLOSE THE TWO BRIDGES** AND TO HOLD THEM UNTIL THE RELIEF TEAM ARRIVES. THEY'LL SUCCEED!

ALL IS OK. THE PARATROOPERS OF THE 6TH AIRBORNE HAVE SET THE RUNWAY LIGHTS...

I DON'T UNDERSTAND, MAJOR! THE SENTRY LOOKED IN OUR DIRECTION FOR A LONG TIME BEFORE GOING BACK ON HIS ROUND...

OUR LANDING WAS COVERED BY THE NOISE MADE BY THE WIND... WITH THIS WEATHER, HE PROBABLY DIDN'T SEE US, DEN***.

* SOLDIERS OF THE OXFORDSHIRE AND BUCKINGHAMSHIRE INFANTRY, WITH THE PEGASE HORSE AS AN EMBLEM AND COMMANDED BY MAJOR HOWARD. IN ORDER TO KEEP TO THE SECURITY RULES, THERE SHOULD HAVE BEEN 28 MEN EQUIPPED WITH 100 KILOS OF MATERIAL, EACH WITH A GLIDER. THERE ARE 31 EQUIPPED WITH 120 KILOS EACH...
** RANVILLE AND BÉNOUVILLE BRIDGES SPANNING THE CAEN CANAL AND THE RIVER ORNE. *** DEN BROTHERIDGE WAS THE FIRST TO COME OUT OF HIS GLIDER.

12

BUT WHAT ARE THE OTHER GLIDERS DOING, DEN ?

I DON'T KNOW, MAJOR.

MAJOR ?

SO YOU WERE HERE, LIEUTENANT* ?

YES, SIR. READY, SIR... OUR GLIDER LANDED JUST BEHIND YOURS...

OK, BOYS.

THE SURPRISE EFFECT WORKED, MAJOR. WE EVEN TOOK A GERMAN MACHINE GUN MG34 WITH ITS MAGAZINE...

BUT BROTHERIDGE IS SEVERELY INJURED.

DEN ! OH, MY GOD !

ALL THESE YEARS OF TRAINING TO GET READY FOR THIS MISSION... AND IN A FEW SECONDS...

* LIEUTENANT WOOD.

13

HAVE YOU HEARD FROM THE RIVER ? WHERE ARE THE OTHER GLIDERS ?

NO, NOTHING YET.

THERE WEREN'T ANY EXPLOSIVES UNDER THE BRIDGE, JOHN. THE BRIDGE SHOULD HAVE BLOWN UP BUT THE EXPLOSIVES WERE MISSING ! WE ONLY REMOVED THE FIRING MECHANISM.

PERFECT! OUR MEN CONTROL BOTH SIDES OF THE BRIDGE OVER THE CANAL. THE "HAM" MISSION HAS BEEN ACCOMPLISHED.

A MESSAGE HAS JUST COME IN. IT SAYS "WE TOOK THE BRIDGE* WITHOUT A SINGLE SHOT".

HAM AND JAM ! THE D COMPANY HAS JUST SUCCEEDED... SEND OUT THE MESSAGE IMMEDIATELY. HAM AND JAM! AND CONTINUE UNTIL YOU RECEIVE A REPLY !

AND WHAT ARE THE ORDERS NOW, MAJOR ?

HOLD THE BRIDGES UNTIL THE BACKUP ARRIVES, AND IT'S NOT GONNA BE THAT EASY AS THE GERMANS AREN'T THAT FAR AWAY... AND OUR RELIEF TEAM WILL LAND ON THE BEACH ONLY AROUND 7H30...

WE NEED TO HOLD THE BRIDGE NO MATTER WHAT, GUYS! THE ENEMY WILL REACT, WE KNOW IT. BUT WE SAW OUR PARATROOPERS JUMP OVER RANVILLE... WE WON'T BE ALONE MUCH LONGER...

WHAT TIME IS IT, TOMMY ?

ALMOST 2 O'CLOCK.

* BRIDGE OVER RIVER ORNE

14

HAVE YOU SEEN ALL THE LIGHTS OVER THERE ON THE COAST GUYS ? THE PLANES HAVE STARTED TO BOMB... WHAT TIME IS IT PAUL ?

HALF PAST FIVE... OH, LOOK OVER THERE, ON THE RIGHT, OUT AT SEA: THE MARINES HAVE JUST ENTERED THE SCENE... BUT THE GERMAN ARE COUNTERING !

YOU BET ! THEY HAVE THE ENTIRE SEA AS A TARGET, AND THEIR DCA HAS ALSO TO CONCENTRATE ON OUR PLANES... BUT... AREN'T YOU AFRAID ALL OF A SUDDEN ?

WELL YES OF COURSE ! BUT WE'RE GONNA MAKE IT !

THE GERMANS HAVE DRIVEN IN STAKES WITH MINES FIXED ON THEM. THE BARGES ARE GOING TO HAVE TO DISEMBARK YOU QUITE FAR FROM THE SHORE. ONCE ON THE BEACH, RUN! THE SPECIAL SAPPER UNITS OF THE EAST YORKSHIRE REGIMENT WILL LAND A FEW MINUTES BEFORE YOU TO CLEAR THE BEACH...

SPECIAL TANKS WILL LAND AT 7H25, THAT IS TWENTY-FIVE MINUTES BEFORE YOU, IN ORDER TO OPEN UP A WAY THROUGH THE MINES.

THE MARINES HAVE STOPPED SHOOTING. THE FIRST SAPPERS MUST HAVE A FOOT ON THE BEACH. IT'S 7H40, TIME TO GET ON THE BRIDGE MEN...

15

QUICKLY GUYS! QUICKLY ! ANOTHER FIFTY METERS !

WITH THE WEIGHT OF OUR WET BAGS AND CLOTHES, WE'RE NOT THERE YET! IT'S GONNA BE THE END FOR ALL OF US!

QUICK, A NURSE ! THE COMMANDER HAS BEEN HIT !

16

PFF! YESTERDAY ON THE PHOTOGRAPHS, WE COULD CLEARLY SEE OUR TARGETS... THE BOMBING HAS TOTALLY CHANGED THE AREA'S GEOGRAPHY...

PAW

PAW

TACTAC TAC

WE LEFT THE BARGE TWENTY MINUTES AGO. IS EVERYBODY HERE?

THEY DON'T HAVE ANY OFFICERS ANYMORE...

NO ONE IS MISSING COMMANDER. HOWEVER, A MORTAR SHELL FELL RIGHT IN THE MIDDLE OF ANOTHER FRENCH SECTION WHEN THEY LANDED ON THE BEACH.

THERE'S A WOUNDED MAN OVER THERE COMMANDER, HE'S GONNA BE HIT. SHALL WE GO GET HIM?

NO WAY! I FORBID YOU! OUR MISSION GOES FIRST! THE NURSES ARE HERE TO TAKE CARE OF HIM!

LEAVE YOUR BAGS HERE. WE'LL ONLY HAVE TO CARRY OUR GUNS AND AMMUNITION FOR THE ATTACK OF THE FORTIFIED AREAS...

BRAOUMM

ZIIP

ZIIP

PAW

17

WE HAVE TO SURROUND THIS HOUSE AND HOLD IT, MAJOR... THE SAPPERS WERE SUPPOSED TO TAKE CARE OF IT AFTER THEY CLEANED IT UP, BUT THEY NEVER GOT AROUND TO IT... YOU'LL BE ABLE TO CONTINUE YOUR ROUTE ACROSS TOWN ONLY AFTER THE GERMAN DEFENSE HAS BEEN REDUCED.

THE TROOP IS ALREADY THERE. BE CAREFUL NOT TO SHOOT ANOTHER FRENCH GUY...

CAREFUL, GUYS ! THERE ARE STILL A FEW SNIPERS AROUND...

PAW

zip

PAW

18

HOW ARE YOU PAUL ?

ALL RIGHT, COMMANDER. IT'S ONLY A SMALL SCRATCH...

BAOUM

PAW PAW

TATATA

TA TA TA

THEY'RE SHOOTING AT US WITH GUNS AND MORTARS ! THEY'RE HIDING BETWEEN THE HOUSES OR BEHIND LOW WALLS...

TA TATATA

BAOUM

?!

HERE, TASTE THIS CALVA, LAD! I'M SURE YOU'LL LIKE IT...

SORRY, GUYS, BUT WE HAVE TO GO. OUR JOB ISN'T DONE YET. WE HAVE TO GO FORWARD AND CONTINUE CLEANING UP THE HOUSES...

BRRRRRR

AH! THE CENTURION TANK WE WERE PROMISED. WE'RE GONNA NEED IT FOR THE CASINO.

HEY! CAREFUL, THE HOUSES ARE FULL OF GERMANS.

GIVE ME A GUN AND LET ME LEAD... I'M NO NOVICE! I DID ALL OF THE OTHER WAR...*

ONE SECTION WILL FOLLOW THE HOUSES ON THE LEFT, ANOTHER THE HOUSES ON THE RIGHT.

BE CAREFUL ON THE RIGHT! THERE'S A RUINED HOUSE, A HEAVY MACHINE GUN STATION COULD SEE US ON THE WAY...

WHY ISN'T THE TANK WITH US ANYMORE, COMMANDER?

HE WENT WITH THE BRITISH FOR WHICH WE'RE OPENING THE LEAD, JEAN...

* PAUL LEFEBVRE, MARKET GARDENER IN OUISTREHAM.

20

THE BARBED WIRE NETWORK CIRCLING THE CASINO* MUST BE FULL OF MINES. WE WON'T BE ABLE TO CROSS IT WITH THE MEANS WE'VE GOT.

ESPECIALLY GIVEN THAT OUR BAN-GALORES** WERE WET DURING THE LANDING. THEY CAN'T BE USED.

WE HAVE TO FIND A DEAD ANGLE IF WE WANT TO CUT ALL THE WIRES WITH OUR PLIERS... BUT THE AREA DOESN'T SEEM PASSABLE...

TA TA TA TA TA TA TA

BRAOUM

QUICK ! LET'S GET OUT OF HERE !

WHAT ARE YOU DOING GUY ?

I WENT FOR THE CHAPLAIN FOR...

GIVE IT UP ! MARC IS DEAD AND THE ENEMY HAS TAKEN THE FIRST FLOOR.

BE CAREFUL! THIS HOUSE IS FULL OF SNIPERS. THEY HAVE BRICKED UP THE WINDOWS AND BUILT REAL ARROW SLITS.

* THE GERMAN HAD MADE A BLOCKHOUSE OUT OF THE CASINO IN OCTOBER 1942.
** TUBES PACKED WITH EXPLOSIVES TO BLOW UP THE BARBED WIRES.

21

BAOUM

WE'RE RUNNING OUT OF AMMUNITION, SERGEANT... IT WOULD BE GOOD IF ONE OF THE CENTURION TANKS CAME TO GIVE US A HAND...

I WOULD LOVE THAT BUT THE RADIO HAS ALSO BEEN WET DURING THE LANDING. WE CAN'T CALL...

PAW   PAW

HEY YOU ! GO AND GET THE COMMANDER, BUT BE CAREFUL, OK ?

PAW !

THE CHAPLAIN HAS SOME GUTS! WITH HIS BIG ARMBAND, THE SNIPER ACROSS THE ROAD MUST HAVE SEEN HIM... HE COULD SHOOT HIM LIKE A CLAY PIGEON...

PAW

PROOF THAT THERE ARE STILL SOME HUMAN VALUES IN ALL THIS MESS, SERGEANT !

22

All the casemates are joined together with underground telephone cables. We have to blow them up. I can be your guide...

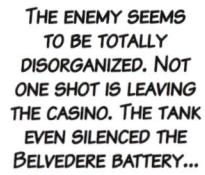

Two men with us! Let's go!

The enemy seems to be totally disorganized. Not one shot is leaving the casino. The tank even silenced the Belvedere battery...

We need to cross the road to get to the casino, Commander...

Commander!

We have received the order to stay together. It seems that our mission has succeeded. The English will follow up...

What are you doing here Paul?

An urgent need... I'll catch up.

ARREUU

?!

DON'T GO FOR YOUR GUN! WHAT ARE YOU DOING HERE WITH THAT KID?

I WAS HEADING BACK TO THE CASINO WHEN... I HEARD SCREAMING... A SHELL HAD JUST KILLED HIS PARENTS... I JUMPED OVER THE WALL TO... TO PROTECT HIM...

ANOTHER SHELL FELL... AND THAT ONE WAS FOR ME...

WHAT... WHAT'S YOUR NAME?

WOLFGANG... WOLFGANG FLEISCHMANN...

DON'T MOVE, WOLFGANG FLEISCHMANN... DO NOT MOVE FROM HERE!

EVEN IF I WANTED TO, I COULDN'T. A SHELL JUST HIT ME...

HEY ! THERE'S AN INJURED GUY OVER THERE... HE'S LYING BEHIND THE WALL OF NUMBER 23... WE HAVE TO GO GET HIM WITH A STRETCHER.

OK PAUL, LET'S GO !

HEY !

WHAT NOW ?

THE GUY... HE'S WEARING A GERMAN UNIFORM.

WHAT ?!... ARE YOU INSANE ?!

HE GOT HIT BY A SHELL WHILE PROTECTING A FRENCH KID... SAVE HIM !

WHAT'S THE GUY'S NAME, THE ONE WHO CAME FOR YOU ?

I GOT TO KNOW HIM AT THE TICHFIELD CAMP. HIS NAME IS PAUL RAPIER. WHY ?

NOTHING... HE ASKED FOR MY NAME, I WANTED TO KNOW HIS...

26

SIRS, THE SECOND FRENCH GROUP HAS ALSO SUCCESSFULLY FULFILLED THEIR MISSION, BUT WITH HEAVY LOSSES.

GO BACK TO WHERE YOU CAME FROM FOR YOUR BAGS. ON THE WAY, PICK UP THE DEAD PEOPLE'S OR THE CASUALTIES' AMMUNITION...

AFTER THAT, GO INLAND TO GET THE PARATROOPERS...

OH GOSH! WITH ALL THIS ADDITIONAL AMMUNITION OUR BAGS WEIGH A TON! WITH THIS BLAZING SUN, WE'LL NEVER MANAGE TO WALK THAT FAR...

OUR COMMANDER HAS 2 BULLETS IN HIM, HAVE YOU HEARD HIM COMPLAIN ?

WHATEVER ! THERE ARE PLENTY GERMANS HIDDEN IN THE TREES OR THE BUSHES, THEY'RE SHOOTING AT US LIKE CATTLE, AND WE'RE NOT ALLOWED TO WALK ON THE VERGES...

AND THAT'S WITHOUT MENTIONING THE MINES ON THE ROAD !

ORDERS ARE ORDERS ETIENNE ! SAME FOR THE NON-COMMISSIONED OFFICERS! YOU SAW IT JUST BEFORE, IN THE PARK, THE COLONEL DAWSON...

LYING DOWN IN A BLANKET WITH 2 BULLETS IN HIM, HE WAS STILL FIGHTING...

FALL DOWN !

27

DID YOU SEE HOW WE GOT CLEANED OUT!

SAINT AUBIN D'ARQUENAY DOESN'T EXIST ANYMORE, BOY! ALL THIS ALSO COST US A LOT... BUT IT WAS WORTH IT!

TWO KILOMETERS BEFORE BÉNOUVILLE... THE DEEPER WE GET INLAND, THE FEWER SNIPERS THERE ARE...

DON'T GET NEAR TO THAT HELMET, GUYS! THE GERMANS OFTEN PUT BOOBY-TRAPS* IN THEM.

BE CAREFUL! THE GERMANS DON'T LET GO OF ANYTHING IN BÉNOUVILLE...

TATATATA TATATATA

I NEED TWO BRENS** AIMED AT THAT STEEPLE! AND TWO VOLUNTEERS IN THAT CHURCH TO GET RID OF THAT GUNMAN!

PAW
PAW

TATATATATA
TATATATA

TATATATA
BAOUUMM!

* EXPLOSIVE TRAPS
** MACHINE GUNS

28

WE'RE ALMOST IN AMFREVILLE BUT THESE BASTARDS ARE HOLDING ON... DON'T MISS THEM PAUL !

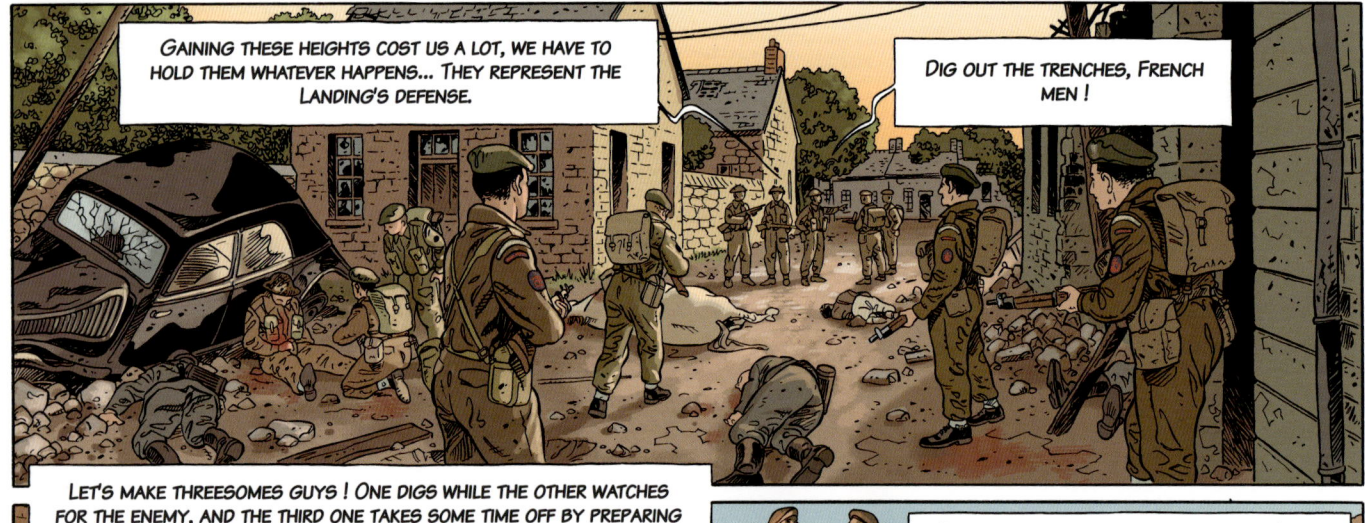

GAINING THESE HEIGHTS COST US A LOT, WE HAVE TO HOLD THEM WHATEVER HAPPENS... THEY REPRESENT THE LANDING'S DEFENSE.

DIG OUT THE TRENCHES, FRENCH MEN !

LET'S MAKE THREESOMES GUYS ! ONE DIGS WHILE THE OTHER WATCHES FOR THE ENEMY, AND THE THIRD ONE TAKES SOME TIME OFF BY PREPARING SOMETHING ON THE ALCOHOL STOVE.

GUY, PREPARE A QUICK PLAN OF OUR POSITION FOR THE COLONEL AND... IF YOU COULD ALSO RENEW MY BANDAGES...

30

IT'S THE ENGLISH !!!

HOURRAY !
HOURRAY FOR THE
ENGLISH !!!

THERE YOU ARE KAREN... THAT'S THE WHOLE STORY... WELL, WHAT I KNOW ABOUT IT, AT LEAST...

SO THAT'S HOW GRANDPA AND PAUL MET?

BUT HOW DID THEY FIND EACH OTHER AFTERWARDS?

IN 1961 KAREN....

IN 1945, I GOT BACK HOME, IN MARBURG AM MAIN... I CAME BACK TO MY FAMILY AND I NEEDED SPECIAL CARE...

.... BUT MY LEG INJURY DIDN'T GET BETTER... ONE DAY A DOCTOR TOLD ME THAT I WOULD NEVER BE ABLE TO WALK AGAIN WITHOUT CRUTCHES...

THEN, FOR A FEW YEARS, I DID A LOT OF RESEARCH TO FIND THAT GUY, THAT PAUL RAPIER...

I DIDN'T HAVE THE CHOICE, I HAD TO SAY "THANK YOU"... FOR ME, BUT ALSO FOR THE CHILD THAT HAD BEEN SAVED...

BUT TIME HAD PASSED... IT WASN'T EASY FOR US GERMANS TO CROSS THAT BORDER...

FORTUNATELY, THERE WAS A REAL WILL TO BRING OUR TWO NATIONS TOGETHER AND FRENCH-GERMAN ASSOCIATIONS WERE CREATED.

IT'S THANKS TO ONE OF THEM THAT I TRAVELLED TO CAEN ONE DAY TO GO TO ONE OF THOSE MEETINGS... PEOPLE WERE TALKING ON A PLATFORM. I WAS LOOKING FOR A FACE... PAUL RAPIER'S.

THERE WAS ONLY ONE CHANCE OUT OF A THOUSAND FOR HIM TO BE THERE, AND I WASN'T EVEN SURE I WOULD RECOGNISE HIM...

32

IT TOOK ME LONGER THAN THE OTHERS TO GET OUT OF THE ROOM BECAUSE OF MY CRUTCHES... AND HE WAS THERE ON THE PAVEMENT. HE LOOKED AT ME AND JUST SAID: "WOLFGANG FLEISCHMANN?", AND HE OPENED HIS ARMS.

DON'T CRY GRANDPA! DON'T CRY!

HE WAS MUCH MORE THAN A FRIEND TO ME, PAUL RAPIER...

WHY HAVEN'T YOU EVER TOLD ME ALL THIS GRANDPA?

WELL! MY STORIES DIDN'T HAVE ANY INTEREST... YOU NEVER KNEW THE WAR, AND IT'S MUCH BETTER LIKE THAT...

AND WHAT ABOUT YOU HELEN, HOW DID YOU LIVE THROUGH THE LANDING?

ME? I WAS A STUDENT AT THE UNIVERSITY OF CAEN. WHEN THE ENGLISH ARRIVED IN TOWN, THE GERMANS BLOCKED THEM IN LÉBISEY*...

* HAMLET NEAR CAEN

33

JUNE 21ST

WE'VE BEEN STALLING FOR DAYS NOW SIR...

YES, AND I'M AFRAID THE ENEMY WILL BE GETTING SOME HELP...

CAEN SHOULD HAVE BEEN TAKEN ON JUNE 6TH. IT STILL HASN'T BEEN AND WE'VE ALREADY LOST A LOT OF MEN...

DAMMIT, NOTHING IS GOING AS PLANNED! WE HAVEN'T GOT ENOUGH UNITS TO START THE ATTACK...

AND THIS LOUSY STORM IS STOPPING ALL THE CONVOYS FROM ENGLAND! NO HELP! NO MATERIAL!

AND NO FUEL SOON SIR...

A MESSAGE FOR YOU SIR... MULBERRY A HAS BEEN PARTIALLY DESTROYED... IRREPARABLE... ONLY B IS LEFT TO ENSURE THE UNLOADING OF MATERIAL...

GERMAN HEADQUARTERS...

THIS STORM IS UNEXPECTED. WE'LL HAVE THE TIME TO BRING OUR TANKS TO CAEN.

THEY'RE GONNA COME AND REINFORCE THE 21ST PANZER AND THE 12TH SS HITLERJUGEND PANZER THAT ARE HOLDING SINCE JUNE 7TH.

MA 2012

34

END OF JUNE. THE EPSON OPERATION IS STARTING AT THE WEST OF CAEN.

WE'RE OUT OF LUCK SIRS! RIVER ODON HAS BEEN CROSSED, BUT WE'RE STUCK AGAIN...

TWO SS DIVISIONS HAVE JUST ARRIVED. THEY'RE HOLDING THE COAST 112 AREA. WHAT SHALL WE DO SIR?

WE DON'T REALLY HAVE THE CHOICE!

ON COAST 112, THE NIGHTMARE HAS BEGUN...

ATTACKS! COUNTER-ATTACKS! WE'RE STALLING, AND OUR NAVAL ARTILLERY IS SHOOTING AS THEY FEEL LIKE IT!

TATA TATA TA

BUT WHAT ARE WE DOING IN THESE TRENCHES? IT WASN'T PLANNED LIKE THIS! WE'RE ALL GONNA DIE HERE...

SHUT UP! DO YOUR JOB AS A SOLDIER! WE HAVE TO HOLD AT ALL COSTS!

35

BLAY, MONTGOMERY HEADQUARTERS, JUNE 27TH IN THE EVENING...

GOOD NEWS SIR... THE SCOTTISH HAVE MADE IT THROUGH THE GERMAN FRONT AT ABOUT 10 KM.

I KNOW... BUT THE NUMBER OF LOSSES IS CATASTROPHIC SINCE THE BEGINNING OF EPSOM.

THE FRONTAL ATTACK OF CAEN WAS USELESS. I OPTED FOR A BYPASS STRATEGY BUT THE GERMAN DEFENSE GOT SIGNIFICANTLY STRONGER... WITH THESE DAMMED ARMOURED VEHICLES...

A FEW DAYS AGO, HITLER ARRIVED IN FRANCE, AT HIS COMMAND POST IN MARGIVAL (AISNE DEPARTMENT)...

FELDMARSHALL ROMMEL AND GENERAL VON RUNDSTEDT ARE HERE, MEIN FUHRER.

LET THEM IN ! I HOPE I DIDN'T COME FOR NOTHING.

IT'S UNBEARABLE ! I CALLED YOU SO YOU COULD TELL ME ABOUT THE SITUATION IN NORMANDY. I DEMAND QUICK RESULTS. THROW THESE AMERICAN PEOPLE AT SEA !

OUR GENERALS ARE HOLDING THEIR POSITION, MEIN FUHRER... BUT THE ALLIES HAVE THE AERIAL ADVANTAGE...

AND, THEY ARE MOVING TOWARD CHERBOURG. LET'S WITHDRAW OUR FORCES TO THE SOUTH AND EAST OF RIVER ORNE AND PREPARE A DEFENSE LINE ON THE RIVER SEINE.

I'M TOTALLY IN ON THIS STRATEGY MEIN FUHRER.

THE SITUATION IS HOPELESS. THE REICH IS STRUGGLING ON THREE FRONTS IN THE EAST, IN ITALY AND IN NORMANDY... LET'S END THE WAR...

NO WAY !

WE'LL CONTINUE UNTIL THE END AND WE WILL WIN THIS WAR... NEW WEAPONS ARE READY... THEY WILL TURN THE SITUATION AROUND FOR US... LONDON BOMBED BY V1S AND THE ARRIVAL OF JET PLANES WILL PUSH CHURCHILL ON HIS KNEES.

36

BEGINNING OF JULY. ON THE ENGLISH SIDE, IT'S A SERIOUS MOMENT TOO.

THE BATTLE IS DEEPER. COAST 112 IS UNTOUCHABLE...

IT'S AS IF WE WERE BACK IN THE TRENCHES OF WORLD WAR I.

WE HAVE TO ATTACK CAEN HEAD-ON AND GO FOR IT... I DON'T SEE ANY OTHER WAY.

WHAT ABOUT THE CIVILIANS SIR ?

JULY 7TH IN THE EVENING.

READY ?

READY.

DROP !

I'VE NEVER SEEN SUCH A BOMBARDMENT. WE CAN'T SEE ANYTHING...

THOUSANDS OF TONS OF BOMBS ! THAT SHOULD CALM THE GERMANS DOWN !

IN CAEN, THE PASSIVE DEFENSE GETS GOING.

COME DOWN ! COME DOWN ! HURRY UP !

IS IT THE ENGLISH ?

THEY'VE JUST TACKED ABOVE VAUCELLES. THEY'RE COMING BACK TOWARDS US.

LET'S NOT STAY HERE, LET'S FIND A SHELTER!

TA TA TA TA TA TA TA TA

37

THIS TIME IT'S REALLY THE END HÉLÈNE! WE'RE ALL GONNA DIE!

CALM DOWN... IT'S SAFE HERE...

OUR FATHER WHO ART IN HEAVEN...

WHEN WILL IT BE OVER MUM?

DON'T BE AFRAID... YOU HEAR ME? THE PLANES ARE MOVING AWAY...

I'M GOING TO HAVE A LOOK OUTSIDE...

I'LL COME UP WITH YOU... WE'LL BE MORE USEFUL THERE. THERE WILL PROBABLY BE A LOT OF INJURED.

AT THE COMMAND POSTS OF THE EMERGENCY TEAMS, SAFETY IS PRECISELY ORGANIZED.

YOU MICHEL, YOU GO WITH JEAN, RAYMOND, CHANTAL AND HÉLÈNE. TAKE SHOVELS, PICKAXES AND STRETCHERS WITH YOU.

TAKE CARE OF SAINT-JEAN EUDES STREET. PEOPLE MUST BE BURIED...

38

THIS WAY ! UNDER THIS HOUSE, I CAN HEAR PEOPLE SCREAMING.

STRETCHERS ! QUICK ! THERE MUST BE A WHOLE FAMILY !

HELP ! I'M CHOKING ! QUICK !

WE'RE COMING ! PLEASE BE PATIENT, WE'RE COMING !

DAD ! MUM ! THEY'RE STILL UNDER THERE... QUICK ! THERE'S HARDLY ANY AIR LEFT...

THIS IS AWFUL... AN ENTIRE FAMILY...

THE MOTHER IS DEAD. THE TWO SONS ALSO... ONLY THE DAD AND THE GIRL ARE LEFT... AND THAT'S IF HE MAKES IT !

THE UNIVERSITY HAS BURNT DOWN, AND WE EVACUATED THE SHELTER AT THE YOUNG GIRLS SCHOOL.

WHAT A MESS !

ROCKS HAVE FALLEN IN THE QUARRIES OF SAINT-JULIEN. GO THERE ! THE REFUGEES ARE TRAPPED.

2H30, SAINT-JEAN EUDES STREET.

IT'S A LOST CAUSE ! IT'S BURNING EVERYWHERE !

DON'T BE NEGATIVE PASCAL ! WE HAVE TO PREVENT THE ENTIRE AREA FROM CATCHING FIRE !

39

LÉBISEY, JULY 8TH.

THE NORTH OF THE TOWN IS IN RUINS...

YES, AND THE CANADIANS ARE MOVING FORWARD... THEY'RE GETTING RID OF THE SS THAT ARE STILL IN BURON AND AUTHE...

CARPIQUET, JULY 9TH.

AFTER THE COUNTER ATTACK OF JULY 6TH, THE GUYS FROM THE REGIMENT LA CHAUDIÈRE HAD TO GO BACK. STILL THOSE DAMNED PANZERS !

A GOOD THING THAT OUR SHERMAN TANKS GOT THERE ON TIME ! WE'RE GONNA MAKE IT TIL THE END THIS TIME.

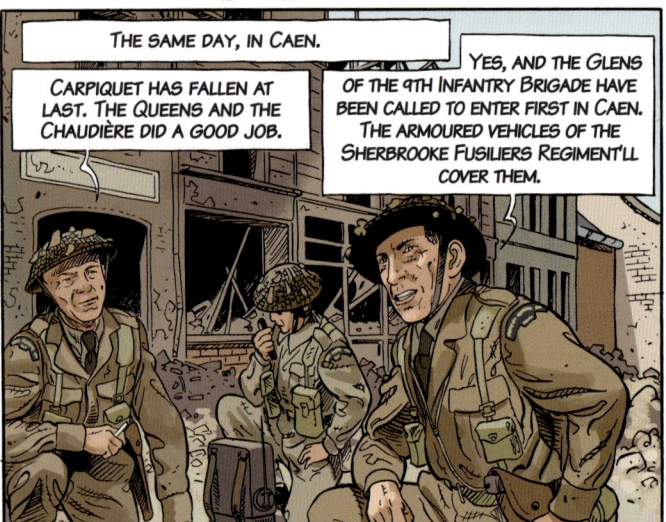

THE SAME DAY, IN CAEN.

CARPIQUET HAS FALLEN AT LAST. THE QUEENS AND THE CHAUDIÈRE DID A GOOD JOB.

YES, AND THE GLENS OF THE 9TH INFANTRY BRIGADE HAVE BEEN CALLED TO ENTER FIRST IN CAEN. THE ARMOURED VEHICLES OF THE SHERBROOKE FUSILIERS REGIMENT'LL COVER THEM.

JULY 9TH, 6PM. ANCIENNE BOUCHERIE SQUARE.

CHEER UP GUYS ! IT'S NOT OVER ! C AND D COMPANIES, GO STRAIGHT AHEAD. A AND B COMPANIES GO TO THE RIGHT. AND BE CAREFUL, THE TOWN IS FULL OF SNIPERS...

THIS WAY !

THAT'S IT, THE AREA IS SECURED. HERE, HAVE A DRINK !

YOU'LL NEED IT... IT'LL PEP YOU UP... YOU'VE STILL GOT SOME WORK TO DO...

40

Even Saint-Etienne's abbey church has become a hospital.

Thank goodness the bombings didn't hit Saint-Etienne...

Well yes, haven't you heard the legend?

No, what does this legend say?

That the British Empire will sway the day the towers of Saint-Etienne will fall down... So maybe they're paying attention when they're bombing...

I heard that the Allies were arriving in Caen...

It's probably true... We don't see any Germans now...

What are we going to become now? I have nowhere to go...

The same for me, my house is in ruins, I only have this suitcase and this old blanket.

Around 2pm...

...I'm the Canadian Lieutenant Colonel Hope. Our troops are moving forward... The liberation is close... Stay here, you're safe, and don't come out before 5pm.

A few minutes later, Saint-Pierre square...

PAW

We're almost there guys! Next step: the junction with the British...

41

IN THE EAST, THE ENGLISH HAVE FINALLY CUT THROUGH THE GERMAN RESISTANCE IN FRONT OF LÉBISEY AND THEY ARE ENTERING CAEN...

YOU'RE HERE AT LAST !

IT COST US A LOT ! THE TOWN IS IN RUINS... THERE ARE A LOT OF DEAD...

THANKS GUYS ! WE ALSO KNOW WHAT WE OWE YOU, AND WE'LL NEVER FORGET !

THAT EVENING, ON THE HIGH SCHOOL'S SQUARE, COMMANDER LÉONARD GILLE, HEAD OF THE COMPANY "FRED SCAMARONI", TALKS.

THE GERMAN HAVE LEFT WITHOUT UNDERSTANDING US BETTER THAN WHEN THEY ARRIVED...

THEY THOUGHT WE WOULD BE SQUASHED UNDER THE RUINS. THEY WERE WRONG...

ALLONS ENFANTS DE LA PATRIE ! LE JOUR DE GLOIRE EST ARRIVÉ...*

FINALLY WE'RE BACK TO LIBERTY AND DIGNITY HÉLÈNE...

LIBERTY YES... BUT AT WHAT COST !

* FRENCH NATIONAL HYMN "LA MARSEILLAISE"

42

By abandoning the left riverbank, the Germans have destroyed what was left of the bridges. Entrenched on the right riverbank, in the heights of Vaucelles, they unleash their artillery on the Allied troops on the other side of the river.

These damned civilians that are giving the Canadians some information aren't really helping us out.

Yes my Colonel... to such an extent that our troops don't tread on the Orne's riversides at daylight anymore.

July 14th, in the quarries of Fleury-sur-Orne...

We've been here for over a month... Will it ever end?

Be brave mum, the Allies will finally arrive... The Canadians already hold the left riverbank of Caen.

I'm gonna become crazy here, staying underground...

We don't have the choice mum... At least we're safe here.

And your sister Hélène, is she still alive?

Don't worry about her mum! Within the emergency teams, it's safe... Well, I hope...

OH!

We need this quarry to continue the battle. Take your stuff, you need to leave. Hurry up!

Schnell! Schnell!

Let me at least grab a suitcase!

Out! Schnell!

BOUM BOUM BOUM

BOUM BOUM

BOUM BOUM

43

JULY 18TH
AT DAWN,
VAUCELLES
AREA

VRRRRRRRF

THE GOODWOOD OPERATION HAS JUST BEGUN... 2500 PLANES DROP EIGHT THOUSAND TONS OF BOMBS ON THE SOUTH-EAST OF CAEN.

SOLDIERS FROM THE REGINA RIFLE REGIMENT CROSS THE ORNE AT THE VAUCELLES BRIDGE TO ESTABLISH THE JUNCTION WITH THE CANADIANS OF THE HALF-MOON.

THIS WAY! FOLLOW ME! WE'RE GOING TO ESTABLISH THE JUNCTION WITH THE INTERIOR FRENCH FORCES ON THE OTHER SIDE...

PAW

HEY! LIEUTENANT CHATELAIN HAS BEEN HIT!

JULY 19TH

TO THE CANADIANS! TO FRANCE!

TO THE CANADIANS!

CAEN IS FINALLY SET FREE IN THE EVENING OF JULY 19TH.

44

WE MADE IT SIR !

IT'S TOO EARLY TO CRY OUT FOR VICTORY... THE GERMANS HAVEN'T LET GO YET...

JULY 20TH IN THE EVENING.

I DON'T UNDERSTAND! THOUSANDS OF TONS OF BOMBS WERE RELEASED, THREE DIVISIONS AND 900 TANKS... ALL THAT FOR NOTHING! THE GOODWOOD OPERATION HASN'T MADE ANY PROGRESS...

IT'S WORSE SIR... OUR DIVISIONS ARE AGAIN STUCK IN TROARN AND WE'VE LOST 300 TANKS.

THE CANADIANS HAVE EVEN MANAGED TO GET INTO THE VAUCELLES AREA SIR. THE RIGHT RIVERBANK OF THE TOWN HAS BEEN SET FREE...

JULY 21ST, AT EISENHOWER'S HEADQUARTERS.

IT'S A SERIOUS MOMENT, SIRS. THE BRITISH ARE STUCK AGAIN.

AT LEAST THE GERMAN TROOPS CONCENTRATE ON CAEN.

TRUE, THE AMERICAN TROOPS TOOK ADVANTAGE OF IT TO MOVE FORWARD... THEY'VE JUST TAKEN SAINT-LÔ.. EVEN IF THE TOWN IS IN RUINS...

MONTGOMERY IS SINKING IN THE GOODWOOD OPERATION, SHALL WE PLAN NEW BOMBARDMENTS ?

NO !

WE BOMB... WE BOMB... WE'RE NOT GONNA GO ACROSS ALL FRANCE AND RELEASE 1000 TONS OF BOMBS PER SQUARE METER !

45

AND THAT'S IT... THAT'S THE WHOLE STORY... MY GENERATION HAD TO LEARN HOW TO LIVE IN CAEN, WHILE BEING REBUILT...

AND IT'S IN CAEN THAT YOU MET PAUL?

IT WAS A YEAR AFTER ALL THESE EVENTS, DURING A COMMEMORATION...

WE'RE GONNA HAVE TO GO KAREN, IF WE WANT TO BE ON TIME AT THE BANQUET...

YOU... WILL YOU STOP BY NEXT YEAR WOLFY?

IF MY OLD SELF IS STILL STANDING, YOU CAN COUNT ON US...

I'M PROUD OF YOU GRANDPA... IT'S THANKS TO PEOPLE LIKE YOU AND THE RAPIER'S THAT FRANCE AND GERMANY FINALLY BECAME THE BEST FRIENDS IN THE WORLD...

COLOURS: CATHERINE MOREAU ; SCRIPT: JEAN-BLAISE DJIAN AND ISABELLE BOURNIER ; DRAWING: BRUNO MARIVAIN

46

NORMANDY JUNE 44

A DOSSIER FROM **ISABELLE BOURNIER**

Arrival of reinforcements on Sword Beach. Seen from behind, Bill Millin, the famous bagpipe player.

All of a sudden, through a gap in the smoke, the submarine defence, posts and chevaux de frise covered up with barbed wire, cropped up in front of us. We were there. Bang, our barges had just hit something. (…) Wearing their green berets, the first group rushes towards the beach, but a few seconds before the second group reaches the beach, a 75 mm shell blew away the barge's bridge, tearing down wood and metal… The main question was: "Had we reached our landing place?"

Philippe Kieffer, June 6th 1944

OPERATION
Overlord

In January 1943, two months after Operation Torch during which the Allies landed on the North African coasts, Roosevelt and Churchill meet in Casablanca and plan to organise a vast landing operation in the North-West of France. There are two goals: launch a direct attack against the Reich as well as to satisfy Staline who has been asking for the opening of a second front in the West for several months.

In the Allied staff headquarters: in the center, General Eisenhower, on the right, Air Marshall Tedder and on the left, General Montgomery.

Operation Overlord is planned

Named Overlord, the landing project is first of all handed over to the COSSAC, Chief of Staff to the Supreme Allied Commander, a staff headquarters led by General Frederick Morgan. From then on, there are more and more Inter-allied conferences in order to organise thoroughly the future operation.

During a conference that is held in Washington, in May 1943 – Trident Conference – the landing date is set for May 1st 1944. A new meeting, organised in Quebec in August 1943 – Quadrant Conference – appoints the landing place. It will be in Normandy and more precisely, on the Bay of the Seine, as the Norman coasts are known not to be strongly fortified, to be sheltered from the West winds thanks to the Cotentin peninsula and to offer large areas of fine sand.

Rommel and von Rundstedt are studying a map

Eisenhower is named Chief Commander

Operation Overlord is really confirmed during the Teheran Conference that is held at the end of November 1943. A few days later, General Dwight D. Eisenhower is named as the head of the Supreme Headquarters of the Allied Expeditionary Forces or SHAEF, a new staff headquarters that replaces the one created by General Morgan. Nicknamed Ike, Eisenhower is 53 years old. He was placed at this position thanks to his organisation skills – he led the North African landings in 1942, and the ones in Italy in 1943 – but also for his diplomatic qualities that are essential to command a multinational army. This time, the Allied States trust him for a decisive mission in History: landing in Normandy, continue towards Germany and liberate Western Europe. Eisenhower chooses Air Chief Marshall Sir Arthur Tedder as his deputy and names Admiral Bertram Ramsay at the head of the naval forces. Air Chief Marshall Sir Trafford Leigh-Mallory will command the Air Force and General Sir Bernard Montgomery, all the Land Forces.

Sword and Utah

At the beginning of 1944, the project takes shape very quickly, and the attack area planned by General Montgomery seems to be too narrow. Eisenhower and Montgomery decide to enlarge it by adding two beaches : Sword and Utah. Because of the expansion of the landing area, now 80 kilometres long, the number of people needs to be increased to 156 000 men and to anticipate additional material, especially landing barges, are required. Initially planned for May 1st 1944, the Overlord operation has to be postponed for a month.

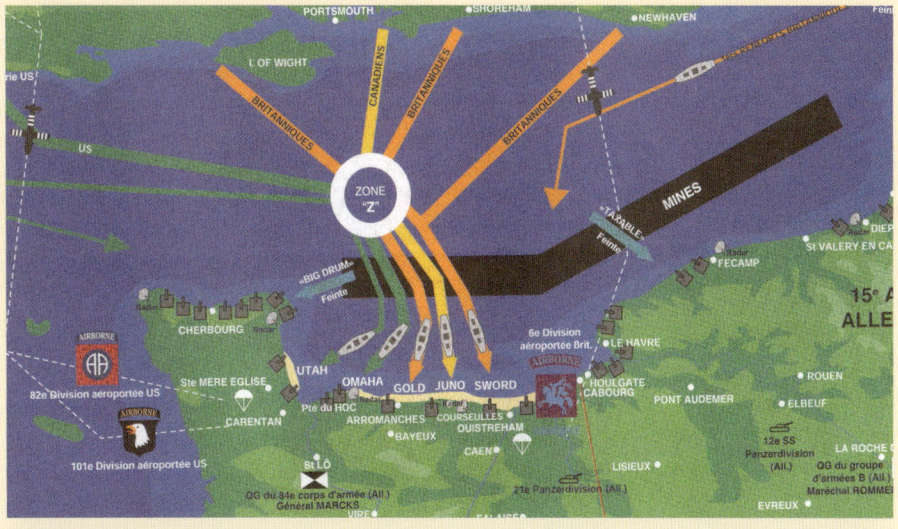

Raids and landings before the *Overlord* operation
August 19th 1942: Raid on Dieppe (Jubilee operation)
November 1942: Landing in North Africa (Torch operation)
July 10th 1943: Landing in Sicily (Husky operation)
September 3rd-16th 1943: Landing in Italy – Salerne (Avalanche operation)
January 22nd 1944: Landing in Italy – Anzio (Shingle operation)

MIDNIGHT !
The 6ᵗʰ Airborne drops on Pegasus Bridge

Commanded by General Gale, the 6th British Airborne division's mission was to place themselves on the Eastern side on the landing area and to take over Bénouville and Ranville bridges that span across the Orne river and the Canal joining Caen to the sea. The paratroopers also have to neutralise Merville's battery whose cannons threaten Sword beach.

Takeoff of a sailplane in England

The 6ᵗʰ Airborne mission

On June 5th around 11pm, six plane-drawn gliders take off from England. Dropped at about 10 km from their planned landing area, they silently continue towards their goal. The assignment given by General Gale is quite simple: "take intact the Orne and Caen canal bridges, in Bénouville and Ranville... The taking of the two bridges, cal-led Operation "Coup de main", essentially rests upon the surprise effect, a fast execution and the determination to win. We'll have to expect a counter-attack and hold until the relief arrives". Succeeding in this mission will be essential in order to enable the transport of supplies to the sector held by the 6th Airborne, going from Orne to Dives.

Pegasus Bridge

Three gliders should have landed near the bridge crossing the canal, three others near the route

on the Orne. The Howard glider will be the first to land, less than 50 meters from Pegasus Bridge. The second one, having a crash landing, breaks into two pieces. The third one lands a little bit further away.

The German sentries are taken by surprise by the 130 men commanded by Major Howard, and who take the bridges of Bénouville and Ranville. Almost all of a sudden, the firefighters cut the explosive charge circuits of the bridge that were installed by the Germans. At the same time, the paratroopers of the 6th Airborne take the bridge over Orne. Mission accomplished! Major Howard passes on the information by sending his famous message

Before they took off, the British paratroopers set the time on their watches.

"Ham and Jam! Ham and Jam!". Now they have to hold until the reinforcements arrive…

Merville Cannons

Around 3am, a thousand paratroopers, followed by about fifty gliders, drop on Ranville. And with them is General Gale's 6th Airborne's staff.

An hour later, 150 paratroopers commanded by Lieutenant-Colonel Otway attack Merville's battery. Otway should have had 750 men and more material but five gliders were lost during the crossing. Scattered during the landing, hundreds of paratroopers are also missing. While some men create a diversion by entering to the North of the battery, Otway's paratroopers attack. After terrible fights, the British capture the German stronghold and blow up the cannons. Arethusa cruiser, placed off shore, is immediately informed of the operation's success. Would it have been a defeat, their mission would have been to shoot the battery in order to have it neutralised.

Aerial view of the British gliders after they landed near Pegasus Bridge.

The Insignia of the 6th Airborne.

THE LANDING ON
Sword Beach

In the night from June 5th to 6th, the Allied aviation pounded the Atlantic Wall defences. A little before dawn, on each landing beach, the naval artillery goes into battle to neutralise the German batteries that are still active. The success of the troops' advancement in the water and their progress on the beach largely depends on the efficiency of these attacks. The 716th division commanded by General Richter and whose headquarters are in Caen defends the area.

Aerial view of Sword beach

The attack...

The day had only just rose when General Rennie's 3rd British Infantry division rush on Sword beach. Their mission ? Capture the beach, go inland and make the junction with the 6th Airborne troops that landed during the night and with the Canadians who landed on Juno. The other goal,

Hermanville, June 6th around 8am

and an important one also: take Caen !

With "funnies" (tanks) in front of them, the attack landing crafts cut a path towards the coast. Together with the N° 4 British Commando, 177 Frenchmen from the first marine battalion commanded by Philippe Kieffer take part in this operation. Once on the ground, special tanks equipped with

HAVE YOU SEEN ALL THE LIGHTS OVER THERE ON THE COAST GUYS ? THE PLANES HAVE STARTED TO BOMB... WHAT TIME IS IT PAUL ?

HALF PAST FIVE... OH, LOOK OVER THERE, ON THE RIGHT, OUT AT SEA: THE MARINES HAVE JUST ENTERED THE SCENE... BUT THE GERMAN ARE COUNTERING !

Hermanville breach, in the morning of June 6th

D-Day's report

In the evening of June 6th, Caen isn't yet taken and the link-up with the Canadians who landed on Juno hasn't been done. The 21st German armoured division launches a counter-attack and reaches the coast thanks to the corridor left unoccupied between the two landing areas. Afraid of being surrounded, the enemy tanks make an about-turn.

Arrival of the reinforcement teams in the afternoon of June 6th

powerful cannons open fire in order to neutralise the bunkers sheltering the defenders and to secure the men's way to the top of the beach. At the same time, the tide rises up and inexorably reduces the sea shore which is quickly filled with vehicles, charred material and bodies…

Around midday, the beach is cleaned up and enough breaches have been opened to enable the arrival of supplies and the landing of the reinforcements.

Disorganised, the Germans have a weak resistance towards the attackers. However, snipers will hinder the way of the troops wanting to go inland.

Objective Caen !

While Major Kieffer's men take the casino that had been turned

into a fortress, the 3rd British division, supported by armoured vehicles, goes inland. Their mission is to control the German strongholds powerfully defended and to take position in the villages before advancing towards Caen. The loss of time at Hillman (Colleville-Montgomery) allows the 716th German Infantry division to reorganise and to install, in the North of Caen, a solid defence line forbidding all access to the city.

On the Orne, the junction with the airborne troops has been done. The bridgehead is therefore reinforced and it prevents the powerful XVth German Army, placed to the North of the Seine, from sending reinforcements to Normandy.

Bill Millin and his bagpipes

Bill Millin (1922-2010) was Lord Lovat's private bagpipe player. According to the Scottish tradition, bagpipe players led the troops to battle, but this practice has been forbidden since the slaughter of musicians during World War I. Lord Lovat disregards this ban and asks Bill Millin to play during the battles on Sword, and in Bénouville, at the time of the link-up with the 6th Airborne.

THE KIEFFER
Commandos

Light and very movable units, the Commandos' missions are to gather information and to harass the enemy in order to unsettle them. Following the success of the raid led on the Lofoten islands, in March 1941, the Free Naval French Forces create their own commando.

The commandos cross a mined area at Ousitreham

Kieffer and the 1st BFMC

In January 1942, Philippe Kieffer, who is at the head of a small group of men, starts an intensive training. He is very soon joined by ten or so determined volunteers,

men became an elite unit. On August 19th 1942, fifteen of them took part in the raid on Dieppe and in March 1944, they create the Bataillon Fusilier Marine Commando (BFMC). A few weeks before the landing, the 1st BFMC, composed of two battle troops and half a support troop (K-guns), is assigned to the No 4 Commando of Lieutenant-Colonel Dawson, himself part of the 1st Special Service Brigade commanded by Lord Lovat.

The landing area is exposed

At the end of May, the 1st BFMC is isolated at the Titchfield camp, in the South of England and are

been changed on the maps, some commandos manage to identify the area of the future attacks. One of them testifies: "On the photographs that were shown to us,

who had managed to reach England after huge difficulties and incredible detours. After several months of intense training, these

let into the secret. The men are waiting for the landing on the French coasts with impatience. Even if some of the names have

The commandos continue towards Colleville-sur-Orne

The commandos in Amfreville

fire on the German defences. The French commandos leave to attack Riva Bella and its casino changed into a fortress. Thanks to the support of a tank, the enemy's positions are neutralised. The second objective of the day will be to establish the junction with the Airborne troops at Bénouville's bridge. In the evening of June 6th, Kieffer's commandos have reached the heights of Amfreville. The 1st BFMC counts 10 dead and 36 injured.

some Normans recognised the places. The port, it's Ouistreham; the big blockhouse, is the former casino; the landing spot, it's La Brèche, near Riva Bella… This information runs, rushes and the English panic…"

on the ground, as the British let them land before them.
Avoiding enemy bullets, mines and any kind of obstacle, the commandos run to cross the beach. The amphibian tanks and other Sherman tanks support the Infantry and open

Stele paying tribute to Major Kieffer, Ouistreham

The Kieffer commandos on the front line

On June 6th 1944, 177 marine commandos, placed under the command of Philippe Kieffer, the ships lieutenant, land on Sword beach. Wearing their green berets and heavily loaded, the men go towards the beach, water up to their waists. They are facing La Brèche, five hundred meters west of Riva Bella. In this area, they'll be the first to put foot

Léon Gautier's testimony, "member of the Kieffer commando"
Packed in their landing barges, loaded to sink to the bottom, the men didn't have time to think. They were really scared but they knew they shouldn't hesitate and go as fast as possible, avoiding bullets and mortar shells, when the barge would reach land. (…) The crossing wasn't restful at all because of a heavy swell and of an ice-cold rain that made even the most hardened frozen stiff, but the one hundred and seventeen were so motivated that nothing could put them off.
Extract of "Les saisons de feu"

OBJECTIVE
Caen !

The Germans have concentrated their best divisions and especially powerful armoured units around Caen. The 21st Panzerdivision and the 12th SS Hitlerjugend, which had just arrived as reinforcements during the night from June 6th to 7th, have clearly put an end to the Allies advance and who liberated the city only a month afterwards. As Caen locks the road to Paris, the city becomes one of the main stakes in the battle of Normandy.

Montgomery's strategy

As they didn't manage to take advantage over a fearsome enemy, General Montgomery imagines a strategy by bypassing the the Tiger tanks, real steel monsters whose armoury resists the most powerful projectiles, cannot pass. The battles get deeper and deeper and for more than a month, attacks and counterattacks follow one another on coast 112. The men bury themselves in the trenches for protection, just as they did during the Great War.

The left riverbank liberated !

Since the beginning of July, Montgomery has been thinking about a direct attack on Caen. The Canadians attack near Carpiquet

German armoured vehicles forbidding all access to Caen

southwest. Started on June 25th, the Epsom operation uses important military means: 80000 men and 600 tanks. The English move forward and take a bridge on Odon. But their advance is brutally stopped by a fire barrier through which

whereas, in the East, in front of Lebisey, the British try to drive

The Scamaroni Company
The resistance and FFI Company created in June 1944 by Leonard Gilles uses the name Scamaroni Company as a tribute to Fred Scamaroni, a committed Corsican in the French Free Forces since June 1940 and who commits suicide without saying a word after he had been arrested.

BUT WHAT ARE WE DOING IN THESE TRENCHES ? IT WASN'T PLANNED LIKE THIS ! WE'RE ALL GONNA DIE HERE...

SHUT UP ! DO YOUR JOB AS A SOLDIER ! WE HAVE TO HOLD AT ALL COSTS !

Final battles on the right riverbank

After the Germans destroyed what was left of the bridges, they move back to the right riverbank of Orne to continue the bombardments on the left riverbank since the heights of Fleury. On July 19th, the Canadians led by the FFI's finally succeed in throwing bridges over the river and releasing the other half of the city.

Entrenched in the South of Caen, the German divisions remain dreadful. On July 18th, Montgomery launches the Goodwood operation, using considerable military means, and that starts with a massive bombardment. New defeat ! The Allies are once again

in the enemy lines. In the evening of July 7th, a massive bombardment hits the North of the Norman city, finishing the job with the German defence. On July 8th, the Canadians liberate Buron and Authie while the British finally succeed in unlocking the access to the city by the North. On July 9th, after having taken Saint-Germain la Blanche Herbe, Venoix and Maladrerie,

Canadian soldiers in Caen's ruins

Advanced Health post during Epsom

stopped, on a line going through Troarn, Bourguébus and Saint-André-sur-Orne.

Even if taking Caen was very difficult, it at least relieved the West of the landing area where the Americans moved forward. Indeed, the best German troops and three quarters of the armoured units were concentrated around the city.

the Canadians and the British enter Caen at last. The junction between the Allied troops takes place at Saint-Pierre's square. Around 6pm, the city is liberated up to Orne.

Canadian soldiers pose in front of the Caen roadsign

THE INHABITANTS OF CAEN

under the bombardments

On June 6th 1944, the Allies set foot in Normandy, but they haven't yet won and the arrival of the German rein-forcements could jeopardize everything. In order to counter this threat, the aviation has been ordered to bomb the crossroads, bridges and train stations, mission more or less fulfilled with success.

Caen, the town center in ruins

firemen start a heroic fight against the fires.

In the evening of June 6th, new bombardments are being prepared. They will aim at Norman towns located in strategic communication areas. A few minutes after 8pm, hundreds of American

A sad June 6th...

June 6th, 13h30 : Caen's suffering begins. An incredibly violent Allied raid suddenly surprises the

Inhabitants of Caen while they were having lunch. The bombardiers missed their initial target to destroy the bridges and seriously damaged the town center. Several parts of the town are hit but the damage and number of casualties are mainly around the castle. The emergency services get organised at once. Members of the Passive Defence, with the help of volunteers from the emergency teams, help the injured that are stuck under the ruins, whereas the

bombardiers drop their bombs on the towns that have become main military goals. These bom-

Civilian refugees in the "Abbaye aux Hommes" in Caen

A woman refugee in the "Abbaye aux Hommes" "cloister in Caen

the bombardiers that the place has been changed into a health block welcoming civilians and injured. Life gets organised as best as possible… Saint-Etienne becomes the center of the city as it is spared from the bombs. Welcoming place for the refugees, hospital for the injured, it is also the meeting place for the authorities.

A long-awaited liberation…

The bombardments of July 7th and 18th, a prelude to the liberation of the city, also destroy and kill, wiping out the university and its beautiful library. On July

bardments aren't precise enough as they are dropped from a high altitude so the Allied commandment decides that it has to be done again. It's the British aviation's turn to take off. Since Caen wasn't taken on June 6th, it is on the list of the cities that have to be bombed. Between 2.30 and 3.00am, hundreds of bombs are dropped on the Normandy city.

Refugees in the "Abbaye aux Hommes"

The bombardments follow one after another for a month. Thousands of inhabitants of Caen found shelter in Saint-Etienne's Abbey and Malherbe's high school, located in the religious

buildings of the convent. Not far away, hundreds of injured come flooding to the Bon-Sauveur hospital. Red crosses, made with whatever could be found, inform

2H30, SAINT-JEAN EUDES STREET.

IT'S A LOST CAUSE ! IT'S BURNING EVERYWHERE !

DON'T BE NEGATIVE PASCAL ! WE HAVE TO PREVENT THE ENTIRE AREA FROM CATCHING FIRE !

Evacuated injured people by the assistance teams

9th, one month after the landing, Caen's left riverbank is liberated! The inhabitants who hadn't left the city welcome their liberators with feelings, but too many sufferings and grief prevent joyous outcries. 75% of the city has been destroyed. There are 2500 dead. Late in the afternoon, a patriotic ceremony is organised at the abbey's square. The small assembly, in which the FFIs from the Scamaroni Company can be seen, start singing the "Marseillaise" with feelings, while a French flag quickly hoisted, blows in the wind.

The emergency teams

The emergency volunteers are mainly young students, like Jean-Marie Girault, former mayor of Caen, who help the people who have been hit by the bombardments. Their various tasks, helping the injured under the ruins, burial of the dead but also supplying the disaster victims, that are often trapped during the bombardments, at the risk of their lives.

THE REFUGEES
in the quarries

As soon as the first aerial bombardments started, whole families drift away from the North of France. Some go south, whereas others rather go for shelter in the quarries of Fleury, Carpiquet or Mondeville. The refugees rush on the road, carrying mattresses, blankets and a few kitchen utensils – without leaving behind their domestic animals.

Petites-Boucheries square in Caen

Feeding the refugees

From June 6th, people start arriving in the quarries. In total, 20000 refugees will stay there, some for two months, others only for a few days. Civilians try to have a normal life underground, but the situation is difficult. The first worry is finding the food every day for thousands of people. Collective kitchens are set up very quickly. Supply errands are organised to go and get the dead animals killed by the bombardments, to go and pick up vegetables in the abandoned gardens or they risk it and go to Caen's train station for flour and military biscuits in the bombarded wagons. Cooking pots are installed at the entrance of the quarries to avoid them getting smoked out, and there is a control on an equal distribution.

Rough-and-ready conveniences

Comfort and hygiene are at their strict minimum. The refugees, living in darkness with acetylene lamps, candles and oil lamps as their only light, are forced to live close to each other with a lack of intimacy. Men, women and children sleep on the mattresses they carried when they left the city, or on straw and protect themselves against the cold and humidity as they can. Living together can quickly become awkward when the outdoor toilets are out of service because of the bombardments or when newborns cry all night. Despite these inconveniences, a strong and honest solidarity is built between the civilians stuck underground.

Refugees in Saingt's quarry at the liberation

Woman cooking a meal in the health block in Saint-Etienne

From forced evacuations...
to the liberation

The long wait for the liberation, during which the refugees kept busy by playing cards, chess, sewing, etc, could have been bearable if there hadn't been the forced evacuations. On June 14th, Caen's mayor together with the prefect order the town's evacuation, forced to do it by the Germans. 12000 people are chased from Fleury's quarry and are sent on the roads. One month later, the Occupying Forces command the evacuation of several quarries in order to use the underground passages for personal reasons. Throwing the refugees in a deep anxiety, forcing them to leave the little they have behind, these evacuations are badly accepted for these people already weakened physically and psychologically. When at last the liberators arrive, they are welcomed with warmth and relief.

Elderly refugees in the hospital quarry of the Coteaux

15

TO SEE... *To visit...*

Pegasus Bridge Memorial (Bénouville)

Carrying the name of the famous bridge in Bénouville, renamed Pegasus as a tribute to the 6th Airborne paratroopers who dis-

played Pegasus as the Insignia of their division, Pegasus Bridge's Memorial is dedicated to the British paratroopers' achievement

when they took the bridge and Merville's battery on the night between June 5th and 6th. Bénouville's original bridge is exhibited in the museum's park not far away from a copy of the Horsa glider.

Gondrée Coffee Shop (Bénouville)

Located near Bénouville's bridge, the coffee shop and its owners – Mr and Mrs Gondrée – were at the front line when the bridge was taken.

Merville's Battery Museum (Merville-Franceville)

As a tribute to the 9th British Paratrooper Battalion commanded by Lieutenant-Colonel Otway, Merville's battery museum offers

a varied and educational visit by showing how an artillery battery works as well as explaining the life of the soldiers living inside.

Le Grand Bunker, Atlantic Wall Museum (Ouistreham)

Set up in a huge bunker, the Atlan-

tic Wall Museum offers to visitors rich collections exhibited with precision. This blockhouse, 17 meters high, used to shelter a Command Post and a German headquarter. Thanks to its five stories and to its rangefinder, the bunker offers an incredible view on the Seine's bay on the last level.

N°4 Commando Museum (Ouistreham)

This museum pays tribute to the Commandos who landed on

Sword beach, and in particular to the French Commandos of the 1st BFMC. It exhibits various original objects and documents.

Hillman (Colleville-Montgomery)

This German strength is composed of tens of blockhouses, most of them underground. Partly rebuilt, these bunkers testify for the power of the German fortifications that the Allies had to attack, but also for the day-to-day life of the defenders inside these small forts.

Credits Photographs :
I. Bournier : 23
PAC : 24, 27
NARA : 25, 34
Archives municipales Caen : 30, 31, 35
Mémorial de Caen : 32, 33

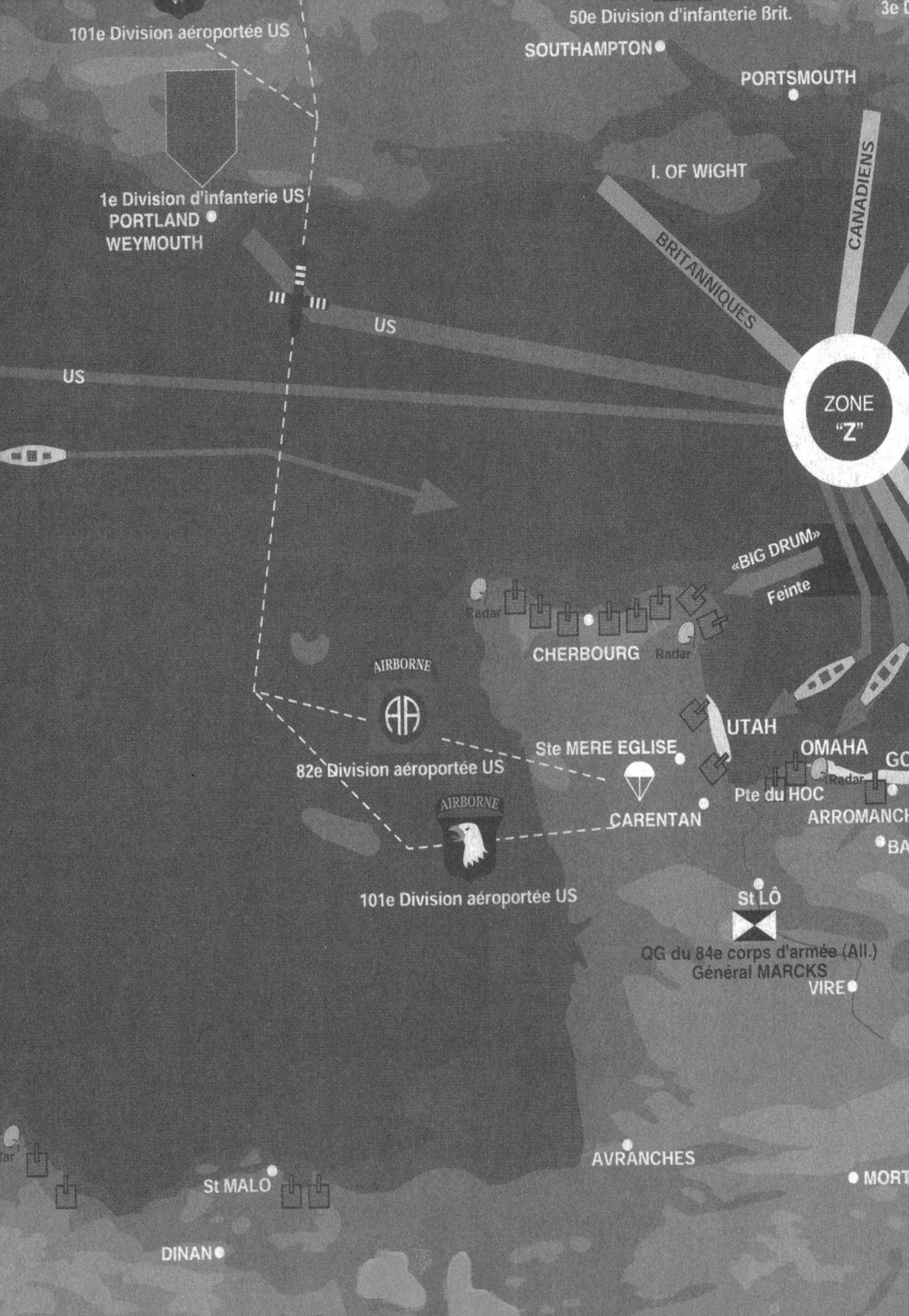